LITTLE OH

LAURA KRAUSS MELMED
ILLUSTRATED BY JIM LAMARCHE

 HOUGHTON MIFFLIN BOSTON • MORRIS PLAINS, NJ

California • Colorado • Georgia • Illinois • New Jersey • Texas

A boy and his mother sat near the window at Number One Pink Petal Lane. They were folding origami paper into brightly colored animals and shapes. "Tell me the story of Little Oh!" said the boy. His mother began:

Once a woman lived all alone in a house in the middle of a lovely garden. By day she worked as a potter, coaxing mounds of clay into beautiful tea sets and long-necked vases as graceful as swans. She passed her evenings folding paper figures. Cranes and flowers, fish and frogs took shape in her nimble fingers.

One night the woman made a little paper girl in a pink kimono. Admiring her handiwork, she could almost imagine the little figure speaking to her. Without further thought, the woman took up one of her brushes and gave the doll two bright eyes, an upturned nose, and a smiling mouth. Then she placed it in a lacquer box beside her bed and went to sleep.

No sooner had she opened her eyes the next day than the figure sprang from the box, exclaiming, "Good morning, Mother!"

"Oh!" exclaimed the woman in great surprise.

"That must be my name," said the origami girl. And so she became Little Oh.

Little Oh was so winsome, the woman could not help but play with her for hours. All day long she frolicked with the paper child and told her stories. They took turns hiding or laughed at silly riddles until their sides hurt. When the woman played her bamboo flute, Little Oh whirled gaily around the room. Each night after tucking Little Oh into the lacquer box, the woman sang sweet lullabies until the paper girl fell fast asleep.

The woman's love for the origami child grew and grew. But her work lay untouched. Soon there was nothing left in the pantry but a handful of rice. "I will make a tea set," the woman said to Little Oh, "and sell it at the market to earn some money for food."

While her mother was busy making teacups, each as perfect as a duck's egg, Little Oh looked out into the garden. "Mother, may I dance in the wind like the red maple trees?"

"No, my precious," said the woman. "You are only a paper child, and the wind might blow you away. Bring my flute here, and I will play for you." So the woman played, and the paper girl swayed and dipped to the music, as supple as a sapling.

When the woman returned to her work, Little Oh peeked outside again. "Mother, may I skip over the stones like the little brook?"

"No, my darling," said Little Oh's mother. "You are only a paper child, and the brook might sweep you away. Come and tell me a story while I work." So Little Oh told a story about a small brave fish who swam a swift river to the great green sea.

When her story was finished, Little Oh listened to the children playing beyond the garden gate. How she longed to run out and find a friend! But she tried to wait patiently until the tea set was wrapped and ready.

"Take me with you to the market!" Little Oh begged her mother.

"I will, if you do as I say."

Little Oh held still while her mother wrote *Number One Pink Petal Lane* on the back of her dress, in case they should become separated. "Now climb into my basket and hide under the cloth. And don't peek out, or you might fall from the basket."

Little Oh curled up in a teacup under the cloth. As she traveled on her mother's arm, she heard the birds trilling and the insects whirring. The smell of fresh-cut grass tickled her nose.

By the time they reached the marketplace, Little Oh had forgotten her mother's warning. Popping up at the rim of the basket, she turned this way and that. She saw people rushing helter-skelter, apples and tangerines piled in pyramids, crickets singing in bamboo cages.

A dog with the eyes of a hungry wolf saw Little Oh moving and loped toward her, his pink tongue lolling. Little Oh ducked down. She felt his hot breath slide over the cloth that hid her. Then the dog lunged, knocking Little Oh's mother to the ground and upsetting the basket. Out spilled the teacup holding the origami girl.

The cup rolled between the market stalls. Close behind it ran the barking dog, sending fruits and vegetables flying. Bolts of cloth unraveled. People shouted.

Little Oh's mother struggled to her feet. She ran through the market calling desperately to her daughter, but her voice was lost in the confusion.

The teacup rolled to the edge of the river, where it stuck in the mud. From inside it, Little Oh could hear the dog nearing. She pushed against the wall of the cup again and again. At last it rolled into the water. By the time the dog appeared, sniffing on the riverbank, Little Oh was drifting downstream.

Little Oh sat up and smiled. "I may be a paper child," she said, "but I got away from the big hungry dog!"

The river ran faster, sweeping the teacup along with dizzying speed. Ahead, a cluster of rocks poked up like bony knees. Careening wildly, the cup crashed against one and broke. I'm done for! thought Little Oh as she tumbled into the water. But she managed to grab on to a piece of the cup and cling to it for dear life.

As if done with its fit of temper, the river flowed smoothly again. It washed Little Oh and her crockery raft ashore on a sandy beach. Little Oh stretched out in the sun to dry herself. "I may be a paper child," she said, "but I sailed the raging river!"

Then she heard a deep sigh. Parting a clump of rushes, she found a white crane standing on one leg, its head tucked under its wing.

"Hello!" said Little Oh. The crane did not answer.

"I'll bet you've never seen an origami girl before," Little Oh went on.

"Does it matter?" replied the bird with another sigh.

"Why are you so sad?" asked Little Oh.

"My dear husband passed away last winter. I miss him so! Day after day I stand here alone, remembering better times."

"I miss somebody I love, too," said Little Oh. "Maybe a song will cheer us up."

14

Little Oh sang the songs her mother had taught her and told some of her wonderful stories. That night they shared the crane's warm nest, lulled to sleep by a tree-frog serenade.

With Little Oh for company, the crane brightened. She spoke of her travels with her husband, of snow-peaked mountains and storms at sea, of grassy plains and golden temples. Then Little Oh played in the sand while the crane waded in the river. Once Little Oh thought she heard the sound of a flute. "Mother!" she called. But it was only the wind in the rushes.

On the third morning the crane exclaimed, "What a perfect day to go flying!"

But Little Oh had dreamed of her mother crying by the empty lacquer box.

"How will I ever get home?" she asked.

"Show me the way, my friend!" said the crane.

The bird unfurled her wings like banners against the blue sky. Up and up she rose, carrying Little Oh on her neck.

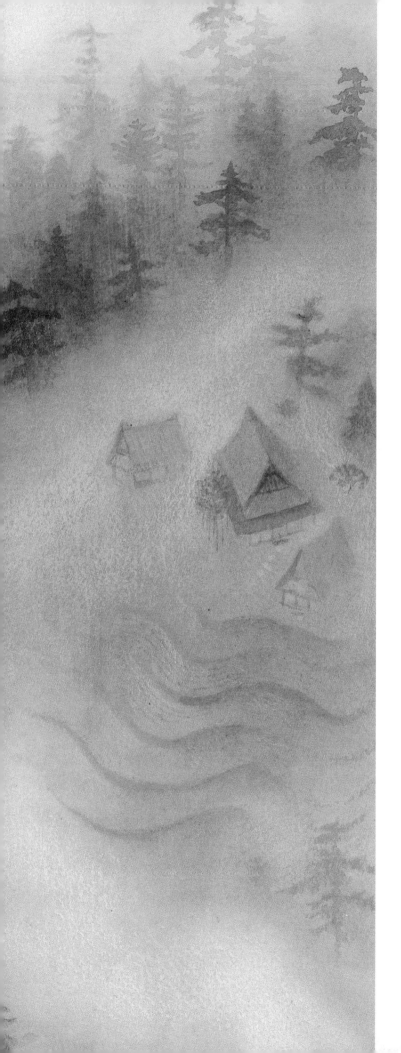

They soared over piny hilltops, farmhouses, and terraced fields. The wind whistled past, calling, "Wheeeeee! Come with meeeeee!" It tugged and pulled at the paper girl, but she held on with all her might.

"I'm flying!" she sang out as streets and houses spread beneath them like a toy village.

"Which house is yours?" the crane called.

There were so many! Then Little Oh saw a lovely garden. "It's that one!" she shouted. The crane set her down and said good-bye, promising to visit soon.

Little Oh climbed a stack of flower-pots to look through the window. Inside, a man and a small boy were writing on sheets of rice paper. Patiently, the man showed the boy how to form the flowing characters.

This was not her house, but a different one in another garden! How would she find her mother now?

That evening Little Oh made a moss bed in an empty watering can. There she slept for several nights. During the days she watched the kind man and his young son coming and going, laughing and studying, and eating noodle soup. Just as Little Oh had no lively brother to play with, nor a patient father to teach her to write characters with brush and ink, they had no wife or mother to tell them stories and sing them sweetly to sleep. And neither do I, thought Little Oh. A small tear rolled down her cheek.

Suddenly Little Oh remembered the house number on her back. I am a paper child, she thought, and I can be whatever I wish! She folded herself carefully into the shape of a heart.

The paper heart fluttered down near the front door, where it lay waiting for someone to come out and find it. But no one did. Up in the sky, gray clouds gathered and a drizzle of rain fell. Little Oh felt herself growing limp on the damp ground.

Just when she feared she would surely melt away, the door flew open and out dashed the boy on his way to school. He picked up the paper heart and handed it to his father. "A message for you!" he teased. The man turned it over and read the smudged writing.

"Number One Pink Petal Lane," he said. "That's just around the corner."

The man walked his son to school, then knocked at Number One Pink Petal Lane. Little Oh's mother opened the door. She moved slowly, her shoulders bent with grief for her lost origami daughter.

Bowing, the man held out the paper heart. The woman reached for it. As their fingers met, the heart vanished, and before their amazed eyes appeared a *real* little girl.

No one was more astonished than the girl herself, who spun around laughing, then shouted, "I'm Little Oh, Mother!" and danced into the woman's arms.

"You know the rest," said the mother, sitting by the window with her son. "The man and woman fell in love and married, and Little Oh and the boy became sister and brother. As for the white crane, she built her nest on their rooftop above the beautiful garden that the whole family tends together."

Smoothing the boy's hair, the woman concluded, "And now my telling is over, though the story is far from done."

The boy smiled at his mother and father. Then he stood up and stretched and ran outside to play with Little Oh.

*F*or my mother, Dorothy Krauss,
in memory of her verve, her wit,
her sense of style, her cooking nonpareil,
and, most of all, her love
—LKM

*F*or John, Connie, Jean, and Jeff
with special thanks to
Karen Adachi and Rochelle Lum
—JLaM

The author and artist wish to thank Junko Yokota
for her invaluable help.

Liquitex acrylic paints and Berol Prismacolor colored pencils
were used for the full-color illustrations.
The text type is 16-point Goudy Old Style.

Little Oh, by Laura Krauss Melmed, illustrations by Jim
LaMarche. Text copyright © 1997 by Laura Krauss Melmed.
Illustrations copyright © 1997 by Jim La Marche. Reprinted by
arrangement with HarperCollins Children's Books, a division
of HarperCollins Publishers, Inc. All rights reserved.

Houghton Mifflin Edition, 2001

Printed in the U. S. A.

ISBN: 0-618-06244-0

3456789-B-06 05 04 03 02 01